LONG DISTANCE GOODNIGHT KISSES

LONG DISTANCE GOODNIGHT KISSES

ANN M. HUGHES

Copyright © 2014
Long Distance Goodnight Kisses
Performance Publishing Group, McKinney, Texas

All Worldwide Rights Reserved, McKinney, Texas. All rights reserved. No part of this publication may be reproduced, stored in a retrieval system or transmitted, in any form or by any means, electronic, mechanical, recorded, photocopied, or otherwise, without the prior written permission of the copyright owner, except by a reviewer who may quote brief passages in a review.

Dedication

To my Chicken. It's hard to believe you are all grown up and off to college.
I am so proud of you and the uniquely kind and wonderful person you are.
You will do great things in this world.

You are never too old for a long distance goodnight kiss from your mom.

✸✸✸

And to my mom, for your love, guidance, grace and belief in me as a mother and career woman.
Thank you for being there for Katie when I was gone on all those business trips.
Because of you, there was never an interruption in the love.

You are gone now but never forgotten.
The memories of our time together will last Katie a lifetime.

Katie knew her mom loved her very much but there were lots of times when her mom seemed so far away. That's because Katie's mom had a job that took her to faraway places for business meetings.

Katie didn't really know what business meetings were, she just knew those were the things that took her mom away. But, no matter how far away her mom was, Katie knew how much her mom loved her.

You see, Katie's mom was different.

She wasn't always there each morning to wake Katie,

fix her breakfast and take her to school.

And Katie's mom wasn't always there to pick her up

from school like other moms.

But Katie knew how much her mom loved her.

Katie's mom wasn't always home to tuck her in at night and give her goodnight kisses. Sometimes Katie's mom had to give Katie a goodnight kiss from far, far away. Those kisses had a special name; they were long distance goodnight kisses.

Even though they weren't exactly the same as bedtime kisses, Katie knew how much her mom loved her.

Katie's mom had a job that took her to exciting places. But her favorite place by far was at home with Katie.

And no matter where Katie's mom was in the world, Katie knew how much her mom loved her.

Once in awhile Katie got to go with her mom on her business trips. It was exciting to travel with her mom and ride on planes to see new places and have adventures.

Katie liked going with her mom to work and seeing what she did during all those business trips. When Katie saw her mom working, it made her proud of all that her mom knew about business and all she could do! Katie's mom never said it, but Katie guessed her mom had an important job with a lot of people counting on her.

One time Katie got to go to New York City with her mom. They saw the Statue of Liberty, a fancy Broadway show and Central Park.

And the best part, Katie got to order breakfast from room service! Katie had never seen so many people and such tall buildings before!

Katie also got to go to San Francisco with her mom on a business trip. They went to Ghirardelli Square, a place where they have every kind of chocolate you can imagine! Katie and her mom rode cable cars, walked in the ocean and waved to the sea lions.

Katie even got to go to Mexico with her mom! Mexico was so beautiful. The ocean was the bluest blue and there was so much of it! Katie and her mom went on boat rides, seashell hunting and ate all the chips and salsa they could fit in their stomachs!

But there were also times when Katie just wanted her mom to be home like other moms. Sometimes it made Katie sad when she saw other moms pick up their kids from school and cheer them on at soccer games. When Katie's mom was gone, her grandma picked her up from school. At soccer games her mom had to cheer her on over the phone.

But no matter what, Katie knew how much her mom loved her.

There were times when Katie was sick with a cold and she just needed a hug from her mom but her mom was gone on a business trip.

Katie's mom sent her long distance kisses over the phone and promised Katie she would feel better soon. It did make Katie feel better because she knew how much her mom loved her.

Even though Katie's mom could not always be there in person, she always made Katie feel very special.

Katie knew that to her mom, she was the most important thing in the world.

Katie's mom sent Katie long distance goodnight kisses every night that she was away and Katie knew how much her mom loved her.

As Katie got older, she began to understand that even though her mom traveled and loved her job, she always loved Katie more. And Katie knew, she always came first.

There was enough room for both Katie and her mom's job in their lives because Katie knew how much her mom loved her.

One day when Katie and her mom were talking, Katie said, "It's ok, Mom, I know how much you love me and you taught me I can be anything I want to be when I grow up: The President of the United States, astronaut, police officer, business woman and a mom. I can be anything I want to be because I know how much you love me."